NATURE

NATURE

Marjorie Eberts

VGM Career Horizons
a division of *NTC Publishing Group*
Lincolnwood, Illinois USA

Photo Credits:
Pages 15, 57, and 71: Photo Network, Tustin, CA. Page 29: VGM
photo files.
All other photographs courtesy of the author.

Library of Congress Cataloging-in-Publication Data

Eberts, Marjorie
    Nature / Marjorie Eberts.
        p.   cm. — (VGM's career portraits)
    Includes index.
    Summary: Provides an introduction to various nature-related
careers, using portraits of people working in such jobs as
environmental scientist, farmer, commercial fisher, and camp
director.
    ISBN 0-8442-4380-9 (alk. paper)
    1. Conservation of natural resources—Vocational guidance—
Juvenile literature. 2. Agriculture—Vocational guidance—
Juvenile literature. 3. Forests and forestry—Vocational
guidance—Juvenile literature. 4. Fisheries—Vocational
guidance—Juvenile literature. 5. Outdoor life—Vocational
guidance—Juvenile literature. [1. Natural resources—
Management—Vocational guidance. 2. Vocational guidance.]
I. Title. II. Series.
S945.E235 1996   95-49818
630'.2'03—dc20   CIP
                                                          AC

Published by VGM Career Horizons, a division of NTC Publishing Group
4255 West Touhy Avenue
Lincolnwood (Chicago), Illinois 60646-1975, U.S.A.

6 7 8 9 0 QB 9 8 7 6 5 4 3 2 1

Contents

All Nature wears one universal grin.

Henry Fielding
Tom Thumb, act I, scene i

Dedication

To the younger members of my family, who especially appreciate nature and outdoor adventure—Linda Adams, Martha Eberts, Jane Kelsey, and Mary Kelsey.

Introduction

Nature lovers like to be outdoors walking in the fields, enjoying the beauty of magnificent forests, delighting in the crash of waves on the surf, observing the flight of an eagle, and hiking in the mountains. Nature reveals its outstanding beauty for us in well-known places like the Great Smoky Mountains, the Pacific Ocean, the Colorado River, and Carlsbad Caverns. It also demonstrates its beauty in the hundreds of thousands of local and state parks throughout the United States. And for those of you who wish to have a career related to nature, a dazzling array of careers exists that will let you work outdoors and savor nature as part of your daily job. Many of those jobs are also concerned with preserving and maintaining the bounty of nature for present and future generations.

Reading this book will acquaint you with many fulfilling careers involving nature. You'll find out what it is like to have a career associated with the environment, farming, forestry, marine activities, recreation, and the park service. And for each career you will discover what happens on the job, the education and training you need, the pleasures and pressures of the job, the rewards, the pay, the perks, and how to get started now preparing for a future career involving nature in some way. Throughout the book, there will be interviews of individuals actually working in nature careers right now as well as stories about people who have made significant contributions through their careers dealing with nature. Plus, you'll find quizzes that will help you determine if a specific nature career is right for you.

CAREERS IN THE ENVIRONMENTAL SCIENCES

W e live on Earth and are totally dependent on the quality of the planet's air, water, and soil for our existence. Amazingly, careers dealing with ways to protect and sustain our fragile environment did not truly emerge until after the first Earth Day in 1970. Suddenly, more people became aware of the importance of the environment, and the government passed environmental protection legislation. While progress has been made in cleaning up the environment,

1

much remains to be done. And new careers with an environmental focus emerge continually.

What it's like to be an environmental scientist

You are going to have a scientific background with a degree in a field like engineering, biology, geology, geography, chemistry, meteorology, agriculture, or environmental science. If you work for the government you are likely to be involved in identifying environmental problems or enforcing environmental laws. In the past, jobs in the private sector focused almost entirely on environmental cleanup. Now more and more attention is being placed on preventing pollution.

Let's find out what happens on the job

Your job may focus directly on cleaning up the environment. You might have the task of cleaning up a polluted stream, the smoke-filled air by a refinery, or a dump filled with chemical waste. Your first task will be to take samples of soil, water, and air to determine what the pollutants are at the site. Then you will develop a plan to remove the sources of the pollution. Your job may stop here, or you may be a part of the next step, which is the removal of the pollutants. This involves supervising the crew removing the waste and continually taking samples at the job site and testing them in the laboratory. The final step is to manage the restoration of the hazardous waste site.

The pleasures and pressures of the job

What a wonderful feeling it is to have a job that allows you to make the earth a cleaner and better place to live! Here's a chance to do something about the destruction of the natural habitat of so many animals, oil slicks in the ocean, toxic wastes in dumps, damaging factory emissions in the air and water, and so many other pollutants damaging the environment. While a career as an environmental scientist can be most satisfying, there are some negatives. When you are working at a hazardous waste site, you will have to wear protective gear, which may make your job difficult to perform. Also, you do run the risk of exposure to toxic substances.

The rewards, the pay, and the perks

When you choose a career as an environmental scientist, you have chosen one that has grown explosively in the past 20 years and is still growing. A great number of jobs have been created or expanded. You have a choice of cleaning up environmental problems, preventing the occurrence of new problems, or creating products that are environmentally sound. You can work in the private sector or for the government. The highest wages and most jobs are found in private industry; however, you will usually receive better benefits with a government job. Jobs with the highest pay in the government are at the federal level, followed by state, county, and then local government.

Getting started

More and more a college degree is needed for a career in the environmental sciences. For professional positions, a bachelor's degree is usually a job requirement. Some employers prefer a graduate degree. For technical positions, the hands-on jobs, a degree from a vocational institute or community college is often required. Because cleaning up or protecting the environment involves so much science, you will find it helpful to major in a science, especially a physical science, or at least to have taken a number of courses in the sciences. This means getting a solid background in math and science in high school so you can continue these studies in college.

Climbing the career ladder

If you want a career in environmental science, you will find three times as many jobs for technicians as for scientists. In the early days of your career, you will be out in the field taking samples and directing clean-up and restoration operations. But advancement up the career ladder typically means more and more time spent in management tasks as you begin to supervise projects. Many environmentalists have started their own companies, and you may decide to go this route or become a consultant after you have gained some work experience. There is also the possibility of working in environmental research and ultimately becoming a director of research.

You are probably environmentally minded, you recycle and buy environmental products, but does this mean you should be an environmental scientist? While you are at work restoring the planet, your workplace is likely to be a polluted site. Whether you work in the public or private sector, you are going to have to become familiar with thousands of government regulations. You also are going to have to spend considerable time writing reports and documenting your work. And of course, you must have considerable expertise in science.

Think carefully now if your concern for the environment lies in being a scientist in this field or goes more in the direction of other environmental career paths like those in government, environmental organizations, education, and the law.

Now decide if being a biologist is right for you

Things you can do to get a head start

The key element on every resume is the experience section. Get a head start on other job seekers by gaining experience through volunteering or serving as an intern. Such a position may be available as close as a local park or nature center. Service clubs as well as environmental organizations will also have volunteer programs. Many programs are open to high school students.

Let's Meet...

Stacey Wimer
Environmental Scientist

Stacey has conducted environmental assessments throughout the country. In her job, she has worked in mud lagoons, creeks, lakes, and other contaminated sites.

Tell me how you got started in environmental science.

During my senior year in high school, I decided to major in engineering in college because I liked science and math. I selected civil engineering with an emphasis on environmental engineering because it involved hands-on work, and I would have the opportunity to work at job sites. I also liked the idea of actually seeing the end product, which is the removal of contamination and having a cleaned-up site. It is also nice to know that you are helping the world by reducing environmental contamination.

Did you need any special schooling or training?

I have a degree in engineering; however, other science-related degrees would provide the appropriate background for a job in environmental sciences. Along with math and science courses, basic surveying and computer courses would be beneficial. Report writing is part of this job, and good technical writing skills are required. I

have received much of my training on-the-job at sites where I worked with other environmental engineers/scientists and geologists. Because a major part of my work involves hazardous material, I was required to take a week-long safety training course. Annually, I take a 1-day refresher safety training course. Federal law requires safety training for anyone working around hazardous materials.

Describe a typical day.

When I am in the office, I work from 8:00 to 5:00 o'clock. On Monday mornings, I usually attend a staff meeting. My time in the office is spent writing and reviewing reports and letters, researching information, and making phone calls. I also take time to keep up-to-date on current technology and advances in environmental engineering by reading magazines, journals, and technical papers. When I am not in the office, I am at a job site. What I do at the site depends on the type of project. Most of my fieldwork consists of collecting soil and water samples. Collecting samples can be a dirty job. I usually wear jeans, a T-shirt, and steel-toed boots. Sometimes, I have to wear a hard hat and safety glasses. My job sites have included a desert, an office building, apartments, swamps, a landfill, a paper mill, chemical plants, gas stations, woods, and a golf course.

Do you work alone or as part of a team?

The majority of my work is conducted as part of a team made up of professionals from my office, the client, and contractors.

How to Catch Fish in a Contaminated Lake

Because of the type of contamination that was present in a lake, Stacey's team had to collect fish samples as well as sediment samples. The tricky part was catching two fish from each species. They also had to be approximately the same size. It was December, and the weather was very cold and windy. The majority of the fish were caught using nets placed throughout the lake. The remainder were caught in streams that fed into the lake. The fish from the streams were difficult to catch because they were smaller and hid around rocks and along the banks. In order to catch them, one person from the team wore a gas-powered generator that had a small electrode attached to a hand-held rod. When the electrode was inserted into the water, a low-voltage current would shock any fish located nearby. The fish would then float to the surface, and Stacey and the others would have to net them quickly before the current carried them away. They all wore rubber hip waders for protection from shock or getting wet. After the fish were caught, they were weighed and then filleted. The fillets were labeled, packed on ice, and shipped to a laboratory for analysis.

Let's Meet...

Rich Walter
Environmental Consultant

Rich works for an international environmental consulting firm handling hazardous waste investigation and cleanup and environmental impact assessment.

What first attracted you to a career in environmental consulting?

My first interest was at the beginning of my college years when I studied civil and environmental engineering and enjoyed the problem solving and real-world application to the environmental field. After 8 years in another field (cross-cultural education), I returned to environmental consulting for the same reasons and also because of the multidisciplinary nature of problems worked on by environmental consultants.

Did you need any special schooling or training?

Although most environmental consultants have a scientific or technical background (chemistry, biology, engineering, etc.), I have found a niche with my undergraduate history training and a graduate degree in environmental economics and policy. There is a need for broad-minded analysts in the field, but you must be able to demonstrate your ability to handle and master technical matters as they arise.

Describe a typical day at work.

Most days I work in the office reviewing data, collecting research, contacting regulatory offices, preparing maps and reports, or coordinating projects with colleagues. However, each year I spend about 2 to 3 months on the road conducting field investigations and research, and meeting with clients, the Environmental Protection Agency (EPA), and state and local officials.

Describe one of your happiest moments on the job.

At a highly complex foreign military base, I was assigned to research the entire history of the site and present the findings to a coalition of local community groups interested in the potential impacts of military activity on the environment of the base and the surrounding neighborhoods. The presentation was well-received and both allayed concern about widespread contamination and focused the community on several specific areas that would require cleanup.

What advice would you give young people starting out in environmental work?

I would advise them to get training in a technical field related to the environment because that will make it easier for them to get a good job. However, the pursuit of a biology, chemistry, or engineering degree should not exclude getting training or internships dealing with broad social aspects of the environment, including economics, public policy, planning, or sociology.

Rich's Favorite and Least Favorite Things

Most Favorite Things about the Job

- When you do the job right, someone's health or the local ecology is protected.
- Colleagues at work have a great variety of backgrounds and skills.
- Work involves travel to new places.
- A new challenge every month is normal.
- There is room for creative solutions to be proposed.
- There will be environmental challenges into the next century.
- Good consulting is based on science, not rhetoric.

Least Favorite Things about the Job

- When you do a job wrong, criticism will come from all sides.
- Field sites, like toxic dumps, are usually in the ugliest part of town.
- Just when you master something, you are off on a new assignment.
- Novel approaches must run a gauntlet of review and regulations.
- Sometimes it seems you are always dealing with the same old mess.

Rachel Carson

It was Rachel Carson who truly awoke people throughout the world to the dangers of pollution in her book *Silent Spring* published in 1962. She pointed out that pesticides poison the food supply of animals and kill many birds and fish and warned that pesticides could also contaminate human food supplies. The mass appeal of many of the arguments in her book led to restrictions on the use of pesticides in many parts of the world. For most of her life, Rachel Carson, who was an aquatic biologist, worked for the U.S. Fish and Wildlife Service. But she is best known as a widely respected conservationist who was responsible for stirring worldwide concern for the environment.

John James Audubon

John James Audubon was an American naturalist and artist. He is well known for his realistic portrayals of birds in their natural surroundings. In 1820 when he was 35 years old, he decided to make the painting of birds his lifework. Six years later he had enough paintings for a book but was unable to find a publisher in America. However, his pictures created a sensation in England and Scotland, and Audubon's masterpiece *The Birds of America,* depicting 1,065 life-sized birds, was published between 1826 and 1838. The National Audubon Society, one of the world's largest conservation organizations, is named for him.

Find Out More

You and a career as an environmental scientist

Take this quiz to see if you have many characteristics of successful environmental scientists.

Personality

- I am an environmentalist.
- I want a career that is consistent with my system of values.
- I like math and science.
- I am a team player.
- I am eager to learn new things.
- I am an analytical thinker.
- I am inquisitive.

Skills

- I have good technical writing skills.
- I can relate my thinking to others.
- I can see and solve problems.
- I can develop creative solutions to problems.
- I feel at home using many computer programs.
- I have a solid background in math and science.
- I have begun to acquire job skills through volunteer environmental activities.

Find out more about being an environmental scientist

The best way to get firsthand knowledge about what a career as an environmental scientist is like is by working during the summer as a volunteer or intern. Here are two programs that are open to high school students that you should investigate:

The Student Conservation Association has summer residential internship programs lasting 4 or 5 weeks for high school students. The programs provide a chance to work beside professionals doing vital work on significant conservation projects around the country. You will learn to live outdoors in an ecologically responsible manner as you help to preserve our nation's rich natural resource heritage. Contact this organization at: P.O. Box 550, Charlestown, NH 03603-0550.

The Sierra Student Coalition is part of the Sierra Club. High school students can join and participate in the running of this volunteer organization that sponsors outings and has action opportunities. Members also get a newsletter, magazine, and access to electronic information on the environment via Internet. To learn more about this organization, write: P.O. Box 2402, Providence, RI 02906.

CAREERS

IN

FARMING

F or 10,000 years, farmers have been toiling in their fields to produce the food we eat. Farmers in the United States have been so successful that today one farmer provides food and fiber for 129 other people. But that's not all farmers produce, they also provide flowers, fish, forest products, food for animals, and fuel. And many everyday products like diapers, paint, adhesive bandages, leather, shoes, and packaging materials come from farm commodities. Beyond producing all these things, farmers are stewards of the land who must treat it respectfully for the generations of farmers to come.

What it's like to be a farmer

You are most likely to own your own farm. Ninety-nine percent of all farms are owned by individuals or families—not huge corporations. And much of the work on the farm will be done by you and one or two members of your family or employees if you are a small-farm operator. Large-farm operators generally have employees do most of the physical work. For some farmers the work is seasonal, while for others, like dairy farmers, it's a constant everyday job.

Let's find out what happens on the job

On a crop farm you will be responsible for tilling, planting, fertilizing, cultivating, spraying, and harvesting. After the harvest, you will make sure that the crops are properly stored or packaged, loaded, and marketed. On livestock, dairy, and poultry farms, you will feed and care for the animals and keep all buildings clean and in repair. You will also oversee breeding, some slaughtering, and marketing activities. Besides these jobs, you must make many managerial decisions such as deciding which crops to grow and when to buy new equipment. You will also have to keep detailed financial and inventory records of your operation.

The pleasures and pressures of the job

Because so many family farms are handed down to or bought by family members, you may have the pleasure of operating a farm that your family has owned for generations. You also have a job that lets you be outside enjoying nature throughout the year.

On the downside, farm work can be hazardous because you'll be working with heavy equipment and dangerous chemicals. Natural disasters such as floods, drought, and diseases that can kill crops and animals are a constant worry.

The rewards, the pay, and the perks

One of the true rewards of a career as a farmer is being your own boss. Your income, however, is not reliable. Whether you'll make or lose money any one year depends on many variables, including the weather, demand for your product, the amount and quality of the farm's output, your expenses, interest rates, and government subsidies. Generally, the larger the farm, the higher your income will be.

Getting started

Purchasing a farm is very expensive. Many of today's farmers inherited their farms from their families or purchased the family farm. Today many young farmers are getting started by renting most of the land they farm. Others are working as tenant farmers. Some government lending programs are designed to help young people purchase farmland in order to become family-sized owner-operators. Another way to get into farming is by becoming a farm manager. These professionals oversee the operation of all or part of a large farm or one or more small farms.

Climbing the career ladder

When you already own and operate your own business as farmers do, the only way to climb the career ladder is by increasing the size of your operation. Many farmers do this by acquiring the land of retiring farmers. The trend in farming is decidedly toward fewer, larger farms. In 1935 there were 6.8 million farms, but by 1992 there were less than 2 million farms. If you opt for a career as a farm manager, you will typically climb the career ladder by managing larger and more complex properties. And you may ultimately supervise farm managers for a bank or a farm management firm.

Now decide if being a farmer is right for you

The number of farmers is declining and is expected to continue to decline in the future. If you will not have the opportunity to inherit or purchase a family farm, the road to owning your own farm is difficult. You may have to spend years renting land before you can afford a down payment on a farm.

You must also consider the very real possibility that you will have to work a second job to provide a comfortable lifestyle for your family even if you do own your own farm. You must truly be committed to being a farmer to be successful in this career.

Things you can do to get a head start

Growing up on a family farm gives you a head start in becoming a farmer. Participating in agricultural programs for young people sponsored by the 4-H and Future Farmers organizations can also give you a good idea of what farming is like, especially if you haven't had any direct farm experience.

Whether you've never set foot on a farm or been raised on one, if you're thinking of farming as a career, you are going to need a strong educational background. Today's farmers have to make more and more complex scientific and business decisions. Completion of a 2-year or preferably a 4-year program in agriculture is becoming increasingly important for farmers. Furthermore, you are going to need accounting and bookkeeping skills to keep the necessary records, and you will find computer expertise helpful in handling all the paperwork.

Let's Meet...

Bill Zehrung
Farmer

Bill grew up on a dairy farm and has been a farmer most of his life. One of his sons is following in his footsteps and is now operating the family farm.

Is a career in agriculture something you always dreamed of?

No, I had planned on being a diesel mechanic, but I lost an arm in a sawmill accident. I completed diesel school training after the accident, but no one would hire me.

Tell me how you got started in agriculture.

I married into a family that was operating several farms.

Did you need any special schooling or training?

I have gone to extension service classes to learn more about different aspects of farming. Each county in California has an agriculture extension service.

Do you use the skills you learned in school on the job?

I have certainly used the skills I learned in diesel school. I have always repaired all of the farm

equipment, including tractors, disks, trucks, and harvesting equipment.

Describe a typical day at work.

My day varies with the time of the year and the tasks I'm doing. Most of the year, I am typically up by 5:30 or 6:00 and out in the orchard before 7:00. If I am disking, I will start by 6:30 and work for 12 hours. If I am irrigating, my day will be 10 or 12 hours long and could extend into the night—even all night. During harvest, my day is always a good 10 hours long. For so many jobs on the farm like spraying and irrigating, you simply have to keep working until the job is done. There is always something to do on the farm throughout the year. In the winter, the trees have to be pruned and equipment needs to be repaired. Also, spraying has to be done every season of the year.

What special skills do you need to be a good farmer?

Today, you need a good understanding of the economics of farming. You really should go to an agriculture college to get the training you need to operate a farm successfully. Also, you should be a good mechanic so you can do most of your own repair work.

What do you like most about being a farmer?

I like being my boss and being able to plan my own time.

A Tradition of Farming

Both Bill's family and his wife's family have been farmers for generations. Bill grew up on a dairy farm, and his father and grandfather were both farmers. His wife's family were farmers in the Netherlands raising bulbs. When his wife's grandfather came to this country, he settled on a farm in South Dakota. Then he came to the Central Valley of California and bought lots of land and put his children on their own farms. Bill's wife grew up on one of those farms where her family raised cows, peaches, and grapes. When they got married, his wife's father put them on one of the farms he owned; and he also put all his boys on farms. Over the years, they have farmed a great variety of things, including alfalfa, cows, beans, registered pigs, show hogs, and peaches. Today, they grow almonds.

While Bill's children were growing up, they worked on the family farm and they all lived in a house on the farm. Two of the four children have kept the farming tradition alive. Their eldest daughter married a farmer and lives on a farm, while their youngest son bought the family farm, as well as an almond-processing plant.

   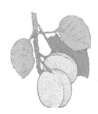

Let's Meet...

Carole Fornoff
Farm Manager

Carole, who was raised on a farm, managed more than 12,000 acres of farmland in Illinois before she got her present job managing 20,000 acres in California.

What first attracted you to a career in farm management?

I grew up on a farm in Illinois and watched and assisted my father in the production of corn and soybeans. My father had a farm manager who worked with him, and I enjoyed working with the manager, too. A vital part of farming is record keeping. Working with my father and the manager in this area sparked my interest in farm management.

What courses did you study in college?

I began by studying accounting and then pursued a degree in agricultural economics.

Do you use the knowledge and skills you learned in college in your job?

The skills I learned in school are used every day in my job as a farm manager. They help me make sound decisions that will make the farms I manage productive and profitable. Knowledge of record keeping, accounting, marketing, crop production, and law is absolutely essential for handling the day-to-day operations of farms. Continued education is essential as well. Since graduating from college 8 years ago, I have taken additional courses and/or training to keep abreast of new technology and crop production techniques.

Describe a typical day at work.

I wake up early so I can review the agenda for the farm operations needed for the day. I then make phone calls to merchants, markets, and farm operators. I analyze the current markets for the crops grown on the farms I manage and decide whether the crops on inventory should be sold. The merchants provide me with prices and recommendations for the fertilizers, herbicides, and seed for the crops grown on these farms. I discuss with the farm operators what work needs to be accomplished that day and during the week. I also consider the operators' ideas because good operators are my best source of good advice.

After my phone calls have been made, I visit farms to ensure that the necessary work is being done and to inspect the crops as well. Crop scouting is critical in order to make timely applications of fertilizers and chemicals. Visits to neighboring farms and farmers provides me with additional insight in making critical decisions regarding the crops.

Tracing Carole's Career

After graduating from college with a degree in agriculture, Carole began her career as a crop scout. At the same time, she was researching farm management firms for the right opportunity. In 1988, she started work with a farm management company as a "gofer." Carole took a cut in pay to get this job and had to do all the dirty work. She put up signs and took photos for brochures. She was willing to do whatever needed to be done to work in farm management for an excellent company. Before long she became a farm manager in Illinois and ultimately was responsible for managing more than 12,000 acres of farmland in the state. Later, she became a vice president of the firm. When a new office was located in Fresno, California, in 1994, she was chosen to manage the office. She manages more than 20,000 acres in California. She also will be involved in real estate sales and client development for the state.

Success Stories

Luther Burbank

Luther Burbank was a curious man who set up an experimental farm in 1893 after working as a gardener and owning a nursery. He developed many new trees, fruits, flowers, vegetables, grains, and grasses. Burbank would cross two plants to produce a third. Sometimes he would cross thousands of plants before he produced a new and improved species. Burbank also improved many known plants and trees. His experiments resulted in many common foods we eat today. His very first new plant was the Burbank potato. He also originated several kinds of berries. One very interesting fruit that he developed was the pomato, which grows on a potato vine but looks like a small tomato.

4-H Program

Learning by doing in an atmosphere where learning is fun is a basic philosophy of 4-H, a program for young people between the ages of 9 and 19. The program, authorized by both state and federal statutes, is conducted by county extension staffs. One of the goals of 4-H is to help young people acquire knowledge and skills in the production and wise use of food and fiber and conservation of the world's natural resources. Each year 4-H members take at least one project to do. A member could select an animal science project and learn about the care and management of sheep as he or she raises animals for market, breeding, or wool.

Find Out More

You and a career in farming

A farmer has to be a jack-of-all-trades to successfully operate a farm. Look at this list of skills, and think about how you would acquire each skill:

1. The operation and repair of farm equipment
2. The ability to work with tools of all kinds
3. The technical knowledge of crops, growing conditions, and plant and animal diseases
4. The managerial skills to own and operate a business
5. An understanding of how to secure loans and credit
6. A knowledge of accounting and bookkeeping
7. Computer expertise

In addition, successful farmers usually share these qualities:

1. An ability to handle adversity
2. Solid organizational skills
3. Good communication skills
4. A true love of the farm lifestyle

**Find out
more about
a career in
farming**

Because farming is a career that requires so many skills, start now to discover what farmers actually need to know to succeed in this career. For general information about farming and agricultural occupations, you should contact:

American Farm Bureau
    Federation
225 Touhy Avenue
Park Ridge, IL 60068

For career information on certification as a farm manager or rural appraiser, write:

American Society of Farm
    Managers and Rural
    Appraisers
950 South Cherry Street
Suite 508
Denver, CO 80222

One of the best organizations to contact for general information about farming is the 4-H. Not only will 4-H have career information, it will also have farm projects in which you can participate to get a real feel for what farming is like. Your county extension service office will have information about local 4-H programs.

CAREERS
IN
FORESTRY

A lmost a third of the land in the United States is covered with forests. These valuable and beautiful lands produce a wide array of products from lumber to drugs and serve as homes for wildlife and sites for recreational activities. Foresters are responsible for the management, development, use, and protection of this treasured natural resource. But they are not alone in the forest; they are assisted by forest technicians. You'll also find timber cutters and logging workers harvesting

29

timber and other forest workers planting trees, removing diseased trees, and building recreational facilities.

What it's like to be a forester

In order to handle this challenging job, you will need to be a highly skilled and trained professional. You will be balancing the needs of people for forest products and recreation with the protection of the forest for future generations. You could find yourself working in such diverse forests as a tropical forest in Florida or a hardwood forest in Iowa. Most foresters, however, work in the western and southeastern states because many parks and most of the lumber- and pulpwood-producing forests are located there. More than likely, you will be working for the government, although there are also jobs in private industry.

Let's find out what happens on the job

As a forester, you will be a manager in charge of maintaining the forest. You will take an inventory of the type, amount, and location of all the trees. If you detect problems with insects or disease, you will have to find ways to keep the trees healthy. If the forest is logged, you will select the trees to be cut and oversee the logging operation. Then you will direct the planting and growing of new trees. When forest fires occur, you will supervise the firefighters and oversee the replacement of trees. In many forests, you will have the added responsibility of supervising recreational activities.

The pleasures and pressures of the job

Being a forester allows you to see nature at its best. Imagine working in a redwood forest or seeing fall colors in New England! On the negative side, you will probably have to work outdoors at least part of the day in all kinds of weather. Your job may require you to spend several days away from home walking deep into the woods. And sometimes, you will work in an isolated region that only can be reached by horses, four-wheel–drive vehicles, or planes. If housing is provided, it may be very basic with no electricity or running water.

The rewards, the pay, and the perks

The more education and training a forester has, the higher his or her earnings will be. In 1993, graduates with a bachelor's degree working for the federal government started at $18,340 or $22,717, while graduates with master's degrees could start at $22,717 or $27,789. Graduates working in private industry received similar starting salaries, but those working in state and local governments received lower pay. The most generous benefits went to those who worked for the government or large private firms.

You will need a bachelor's degree in forestry for a career as a forester. Some states may require you to meet licensing or registration requirements in order to get the title of "professional forester." To become a forest technician, you'll need a high school diploma and at least 2 years of experience in forestry, which you can get on the job or in a community college. There arc no formal educational requirements for forestry and logging workers. They generally develop their skills through on-the-job training; however, a few vocational schools and community colleges offer courses in forestry that could be helpful.

Getting started

Recent graduates in forestry begin working under the supervision of skilled foresters before they become foresters. Then if you work for the federal government, you will advance to supervising a district, then to supervising a region or to a top management position. You also can opt to specialize in an area such as disease control or fire prevention. In the private sector, you will advance up the corporate ladder increasingly supervising more employees and having more management responsibilities.

Climbing the career ladder

Experienced foresters can choose to work independently as consultants. The higher you climb on the career ladder, the more time you will spend in the office handling administrative and management chores.

Now decide if being a forester is right for you

A career in forestry is appealing because it is tied to interests in the outdoors, biological sciences, and environment. Because so many young people want to have a career in which they can play a role in protecting the environment, the competition for jobs as foresters is very intense. To get a job as a forester, you must be willing to get top marks in school and considerable experience in forestry-related areas so that you will have an advantage in job hunting.

Things you can do to get a head start

Learn what it is like to be a forester by attending field trips and camps sponsored by forestry schools. Then get experience during your summer breaks in college by working or serving as an intern in parks or forests or for an environmental organization. If you can't get a job that pays, work as a volunteer. While you are in high school, take as much math and science as you can to prepare for the rigorous college program a forester takes.

Let's Meet...

Dave Dulitz
Registered Professional Forester

Dave is the forest manager of Mt. Home State Forest, a 4,000-acre state forest, located in the southern Sierra Nevada mountains of California.

Did you need any special schooling or training to become a forester?

I attended Humboldt State University in Arcata, California, and obtained a degree in forest management. There are many good forestry schools in the United States, but I chose Humboldt because it is located in a beautiful redwood forest. These forests make a perfect outdoor laboratory in which to study forestry.

What special skills do you need to be a good forester?

You must know enough about all of the plants, animals, and land in the forest to understand how they interact in the ecosystem and how human activities influence the forest. You need a good knowledge of math in order to understand how to measure the trees and other plants. You also must be able to work well with other people, not only your coworkers, but also the visitors to the forest.

Describe your work environment.

I work in a beautiful forest that contains many kinds of trees including giant sequoias. The giant sequoias are the largest of all trees and can reach more than 20 feel in diameter. Mt. Home State Forest is more than 6,000 feet in elevation, so it is cool, even in the summer months. In the winter, we can get more than 12 feet of snow on the ground.

What do you like least about your job?

I don't like dealing with people who damage the forest or are disrespectful of the area where I work. They are the people who litter the ground with trash, write names on rocks with spray paint, drive nails into trees, and otherwise destroy the forest. They also are the people who are critical of the things that foresters are doing in the forest because they do not understand the principles of good forest management.

What advice would you give young people starting out in forestry?

Study hard in school to get a good understanding of all the basic subjects such as English, math, and biology. Whenever you get the chance, visit a forested area and get out and walk through the trees. Try to be observant and notice how the plants and animals of the forest interact. See if you can determine how human activities have changed the forest. Learn about all the beneficial uses that our natural resources can provide if managed correctly.

A Day in the Life of a Forest Manager

Dave leaves early for work each day because it's a long drive to the office, which is in a fairly remote location. The road is steep and full of curves without much traffic, so he can observe the forest and the animals on the way to work.

He almost always gets a few phone calls from people in the morning who want information about the forest. He also may write a few letters or send maps to people who request information. Some mail comes through the computer at his office.

Five people work for Dave in the summer; he must be sure that they have work projects for the day. Some may be working on campgrounds doing routine cleaning or special maintenance. Others may be measuring timber inventory plots or marking timber for sale. Surveying boundaries or drawing maps for different land management projects are other tasks. Dave spends most of his time supervising employees and planning for future projects.

During the course of the day, he will try to visit several areas of the forest and observe how the projects are proceeding and solve any problems that have come up. At the end of the day, he may write some reports or handle special problems.

Let's Meet...

Dorothy Abeyta
Arborist

Dorothy is an arborist, a specialist in the care and maintenance of trees.

Did you need any special training or schooling to become an arborist?

Yes. In college I studied biochemistry, but found I did not like being in a laboratory all day long. Later, I spent 2 years in graduate school to complete a master's degree in plant pathology, the study of plant health. During that time I did field research on trees and found I enjoyed working outdoors in the "real world."

What was your first job?

My first job was with a company that specialized in nursery and landscape consulting.

What is your workday like now that you have your own company?

I like to start my days with fieldwork, especially in the summer because the mornings are cooler. I may visit anywhere from one to four sites in a day. I take tools, a note pad, and at

times a tape recorder with me so I can write or record all my observations. Sometimes I take samples of leaves, branches, bark, or roots back to the office where I can look at them under the microscope to identify problems. The last part of the day is spent writing reports on the sites I visited, describing to the site owner the problems the trees have and the solutions.

What special skills do you need to be a good arborist?

One of the most important skills in diagnosing tree problems is knowing how to use your senses. You must be keenly aware of the tree and its surroundings. Tree problems can be detected with your eyes, your nose, your sense of touch, and sometimes your taste and hearing. Another necessary skill is effective communication. Trees cannot talk or write so I must tell their owners about a tree's problems or needs in language the owners understand, rather than scientific jargon.

Describe your work environment.

Half of my time is spent in parks, on highways, on construction sites, in backyards, and on hillsides. Anywhere there are trees, I may find a job. The rest of my time is spent in my home office working on the computer or telephone.

Meeting an Ecological Challenge

One of the most challenging and rewarding jobs Dorothy has is working on a new development. She makes sure that the existing trees continue to thrive and grow in an area where people want to build homes, parks, and shopping malls. It's a challenge because it requires more than just knowledge of trees and how they work. This type of construction project requires a lot of preplanning and cooperation with the builder.

Dorothy must have detailed knowledge of what the builder wants and the construction techniques and equipment that will be used. She has to know how buildings, walls, sidewalks, streets, sewers, and utility lines are constructed so she can understand what the construction will do to the trees she is trying to save or so she can plan an alternate, less-harmful construction technique. She reads architects' blueline drawings and understands the problems of the construction equipment operators. She must consider how the new building and sidewalks and other construction will affect the trees aboveground and below ground. The reward is to see majestic trees arching over a new park, playground, homes, or streets when a project is successfully completed.

Success Stories

John Muir was such an ardent conservationist back in 1890 that he managed to convince the U.S. Congress to establish both Yosemite and Sequoia National Parks, plus he persuaded President Theodore Roosevelt to set aside 148 million acres of forest reserves. He was also involved in the creation of Mount Rainier, the Petrified Forest, and Grand Canyon National Parks. Muir is often called the "Father of the National Park System." As an explorer, naturalist, and writer he traveled across the United States, Europe, Asia, Africa, and the Arctic. However, California became his home and Yosemite Valley his passion. In 1892 he founded the Sierra Club, an organization designed to protect the environment. His goal was to preserve the beauty of the Sierra Nevada Mountains in California. In his own words, he wanted to "do something for wildness and make the mountains glad."

John Muir served as the first president of the Sierra Club until his death in 1914. This member-supported conservation organization now has 550,000 members and 63 chapters. Its purpose is to explore, enjoy, and protect the wild places of the earth; to practice and promote the responsible use of the earth's ecosystems and resources; to educate and restore the quality of the natural and human environment; and to use all lawful means to carry out these objectives.

Find Out More

You and a career in forestry

Before deciding on a career as a forester, it's important that you be aware of some characteristics that all successful foresters share. Read through this list to determine if you possess most, if not all, of these characteristics.

1. I have excellent health.
2. I love the outdoors.
3. I am willing to work outdoors every day in all kinds of weather.
4. I have the strength and stamina to do hard physical labor.
5. I can endure actual hardship that might be necessary in fighting a fire.
6. I like nature and am interested in protecting it.
7. I am well-coordinated.
8. I like living in rural areas.
9. I can work as part of a team.
10. I am able to supervise people.
11. I can make quick, intelligent decisions in dealing with unexpected hazards or events.
12. I have good communication skills.

Find out more about careers in forestry

The Society of American Foresters is the organization that represents the forestry profession. In its career packet, basic information is provided on careers as foresters and forest technicians. The packet also has a job seekers' guide and a list of schools with society-recognized programs for foresters and forest technicians. You should be able to get more useful information from one of these schools of forestry. To get the career packet, write:

Society of American Foresters
5400 Grosvenor Lane
Bethesda, MD 20814-2198

Foresters and forest technicians are not the only occupations that are concerned with the care of trees and their environment. You might also want to investigate a career as an arborist, gardener, landscaper, nursery worker, or groundskeeper.

CAREERS IN FISHING AND MARINE ACTIVITIES

F or so many individuals, the ocean and working on the ocean holds an amazing fascination. And this seems quite appropriate because the ocean covers almost three-fourths of the earth's surface. Both on and beneath the surface, millions of people have found satisfying careers. Merchant marines transport people and products. Fishers harvest millions of tons of fish. Divers search for treasure. Oceanographers study life in the sea and the land beneath the sea. Now people are even mining minerals from the ocean and harnessing energy from the waves.

What it's like to be a commercial fisher

As a fisher, you are most likely to work on a large fishing vessel that operates in deep water hundreds of miles from shore and is capable of hauling a catch of thousands of pounds of fish. The boat may even have facilities aboard where fish are processed and prepared for sale. You probably will stay away from home for weeks, and it could be as long as several months.

Some commercial fishers, however, work on small boats in relatively shallow waters and often in sight of land. The crews on these vessels are quite small—usually only one or two people. Their stays at sea are just for a day or so.

Let's find out what happens on the job

The captain is in charge of the entire fishing operation determining which fish are to be looked for, where the vessel will go, how the fish will be caught, and how long the trip will last. The captain navigates the boat using electronic equipment such as autopilots, a loran system, and satellites to determine position.

The deckhands work shifts usually lasting 6 hours, with the first mate taking on the captain's responsibilities when the captain is off duty. The deckhands, under the direction of the captain or first mate, operate the fishing gear, letting out and pulling in nets and lines. They also have to wash, salt, ice, and stow away the fish. Plus they must keep the decks clean and clear and the engines working.

The pleasures and pressures of the job

On a fishing vessel you will have the camaraderie of working as part of a team. Plus there is always the exhilaration of being on the water, feeling the ocean spray, and savoring the rocking motion of the boat as it moves through the water. Frequently, however, you'll face the challenge of working in rough seas with high waves on slippery decks where hazardous conditions exist, and help is not nearby. Malfunctioning navigation or communication equipment may lead to collisions or even ship-wrecks. You must also guard against injury from becoming entangled in the fishing nets or gear. Be aware, too, that this is strenuous work that may be very intense while netting and hauling the catch aboard.

The rewards, the pay, and the perks

The major reward of being a commercial fisher is being involved in a lifestyle that you find to be truly appealing. Your pay will vary greatly depending on what your job is aboard a boat, the size of the boat, and the amount and value of the catch. All of the costs

for operating the ship, the repair
and maintenance of the equipment and gear, and the crew's
supplies are deducted from the
sale of the catch. What's left is
then distributed to the crew
according to a prearranged percentage. The ship's owner, who
is usually the captain, typically
receives one-half of the net pro-
ceeds and pays for keeping up
the vessel.

Getting started

You generally learn how to be
a commercial fisher on the job.
Many fishers learn the job from
members of their families who
are fishers. There are absolutely
no academic requirements for
becoming a fisher. You could
accelerate your acquisition of
fishing skills by enrolling in a
2-year vocational-technical
program offered by some sec-
ondary schools in coastal areas.
Also, experienced fishers find it
helpful to take short-term work-
shops at various postsecondary
schools. These programs provide
a good working knowledge of
electronic equipment used in
navigation and communication
and the latest improvements in
fishing gear. If you are a captain
or mate on a vessel of 200 gross
tons or more, you will need to be
licensed. All captains on sport
fishing boats also are licensed.

Climbing the career ladder

You typically start out on a fishing vessel as a deckhand. Then, if you have the mechanical aptitude and interest, you can branch off into ship engineering and eventually become a licensed chief engineer on a large commercial vessel. The next step beyond deckhand for most fishers on a large vessel is to become a boatswain, a highly experienced deckhand with supervisory responsibilities. Boatswains in time become second mates, first mates, and ultimately captains. Most captains become self-employed, and the majority eventually own or have an interest in one or more fishing vessels.

Now decide if being a commercial fisher is right for you

The life of a commercial fisher is not an easy one. Before deciding on this career, you need to be aware of these economic facts: (1) overfishing and pollution have reduced the number of fish, (2) government regulations are sharply reducing the number of fish that can be caught and the length of the fishing season for certain species, (3) technological improvements have reduced the size of crews required to operate large vessels, (4) aquaculture, the raising and harvesting of fish, has reduced the need for certain kinds of fish, and (5) fishing is a seasonal occupation.

Let's Meet...

Dennis Forbes
Commercial Fisher

Dennis is the captain of a 90-foot boat that he uses for fishing for sole, channel rock fish, sable fish, ling and rock cod, and halibut.

Tell me how you got started in commercial fishing.

When I was 11 years old, my family moved to a small coastal town. I was attracted to the water and wandered down to the docks looking for something to do. A commercial fisher took me out on the weekends for company, and I started learning the trade. He paid me a percentage of the catch, and one weekend I earned $110, which was a great deal of money 30 years ago. I've been fishing ever since, except for a brief time in college.

How are fishers starting out today?

They are learning the trade as I did. Unfortunately, there aren't as many boats and jobs, so it's harder to find someone willing to take you out. In general, you have to know somebody to get aboard a boat.

Describe a typical fishing trip.

I have two helpers aboard the boat, and we normally stay out 3 to 6 days depending on how many

fish we get. I make the choice of where we go, what gear to put down, what nets to use, and how much wire to put down. The skipper makes all the choices. My crew has to know how to navigate, to roll gear up, to sew the nets, and to ice the fish properly. We all cook. When we're out, we work 24-hour days and only sleep 4 to 6 hours at a time when all the chores are done.

What special skills do you need to be a good commercial fisher?

Besides understanding how to catch fish, you need to be a good navigator. You should also have solid mechanical skills because there are always repairs to be made from the engine to the fishing gear. A knowledge of first aid is essential, too. To be successful you have to be an aggressive self-starter—always out there trying.

Describe your work environment.

My boat at 90 feet is one of the bigger commercial fishing boats. Most are between 50 and 70 feet long. Our living quarters are quite comfortable: We have a refrigerator and freezer and videos we can watch. Much of the boat is devoted to the fishing gear and space to store the fish.

What is the most difficult part of your job?

I dislike being away from my family so much. This is a 12-month job for me, and I am on the ocean from 120 to 140 days a year.

A Collision with a Freighter

Dennis was aboard his boat, the *Pacific Pearl,* fishing off San Francisco. It was an extremely foggy night—impossible to see more than a few feet. The radar went out so they couldn't tell if any other boats were nearby. Suddenly, they ran into a 600-foot freighter that cut their boat in half and then never even stopped. Fortunately, Dennis was able to get out a Mayday signal so the Coast Guard knew they were in trouble.

There was no time to get out the life raft or get into a life jacket before the boat sank. The crew and Dennis had to cling to a board. They could hear other boats searching for them; the boats couldn't see them because of the fog and couldn't hear them above the noise of their engines.

A coast guard officer on his very first assignment figured how they were likely to drift with the current and started looking for them in that spot. He slowed his boat down when a crew member saw a board in the water, and Dennis and his crew started hollering. The rescuers heard them and then found them.

Dennis was so cold that his legs were too stiff to climb aboard. Later, one of the crew told him that there had been a shark swimming around nearby.

Let's Meet...

Sidney E. Snider
Aquarist

Sidney is an aquarist. Her career grew out of her childhood hobby of keeping turtles and fish.

Tell me how you got started in marine biology.

My career started simply as a hobby. It was something I loved to do. My first aquatic pets were the baby Red Ear Slider turtles that were popular in the early 1970s. I set up my first aquarium, a 5-gallon freshwater tank containing mostly tetras, around the age of 12. In high school I ventured into saltwater aquaria. I kept animals that I actually collected at the coast two and one-half hours away and brought back in coolers, fish such as Sergeant Majors, juvenile Spade fish, and Filefish as well as the ever-popular hermit crab. I began to explore the habitats of these animals using snorkeling gear, and sometimes even collected at night.

What special skills do you need to be a good marine biologist?

A marine biologist need strong science and math skills to perform many of the tasks that are a part of his or her job. In

particular, a knowledge of marine plants and animals—where they live and how they interact—is necessary. Communication skills are helpful as well as an ability to interact well with others, to be a team player. Being certified to scuba dive is often a fundamental part of the job. Most importantly, a desire to work hard and an ability to make sacrifices in order to do something that you love is at the heart of any successful marine biologist.

What advice would you give young people starting out in marine biology?

The best way to decide whether something that you think would make a great career is right for you is to get as much hands-on experience as possible. Fortunately, with marine biology, this is not difficult. Many colleges and marine labs offer summer internships that allow you to get this experience in areas of research that include both lab work and fieldwork. In this way, you are "doing" science as well as "learning" about it. The aquarium where I work has a summer intern program in which students shadow volunteer guides who teach the public about various animals on exhibit. You may think that volunteering is wasted time that could otherwise be spent at a paying job. However, for careers such as marine biology in which there is a lot of competition for jobs, volunteering is often the only way to get the experience that you need in order to compete for those jobs.

Sidney's Day at the Aquarium

A typical day begins between 7:30 and 8:00 so there are 2 hours of maintenance time to get the exhibits ready before opening. First stop is the aquarium's food room where Sidney picks up a couple of bottles of "spooge" (a blended concoction of frozen krill, flake food, and seawater) to feed the anemones. She then inspects all of the tanks and their inhabitants to determine what maintenance needs to be done and to ensure that all of the fish look healthy. The cleaning of windows and tank surfaces and siphoning of debris and leftover food are all part of every morning's routine.

After the tanks are ready for public viewing, the animals have to be fed. This food includes live algae and juvenile brine shrimp which Sidney helps grow in a special culture room. She also feeds chopped squid, shrimp, clams, and fish to her animals.

Afternoons can vary in their agenda, but always, rounds are performed to make sure all animals are "happy," and the visitors are seeing the tanks at their best. Sometimes, she goes out scuba diving to collect new animals or out to the slough to dig for clams, ghost shrimp, or eelgrass. Often she's involved in meetings. Final rounds are of utmost importance and include making sure all life support systems are running and all tanks have water flow before she leaves for the evening between 4:30 and 5:00.

Success Stories

Jacques Cousteau

"Sooner or later man will live underwater and work there," Jacques Cousteau, the French oceanographer, author, and motion picture director, has predicted. Cousteau has invented many devices for exploring under the sea. One was the first scuba apparatus, called the aqualung, which he developed with Emile Gagnan in 1943. Since 1951, he has sailed the world on his research ship *Calypso* exploring the oceans. He also served as head of the Conshelf Saturation Dive Program experiments in which people lived and worked in deep water for long periods of time. Cousteau has garnered fame for his books and movies and especially for his award-winning television series "The Undersea World of Jacques Cousteau." Not only has Cousteau done so much to teach people about the sea, he has also worked to preserve this special environment.

Bathyscaphe

While underwater vehicles go back to 1620, it was the bathysphere built by William Beebe, an American naturalist, and first used in 1930, that let scientists begin to explore the ocean depths. However, it didn't have much maneuverability. Auguste Piccard created the bathyscaphe, which was the first truly mobile undersea vessel. In 1960, Don Walsh and Piccard's son Jacques reached the deepest spot in the world in the bathyscaphe *Trieste*.

Find Out More

You and a career in marine activities

See how you respond to these questions and comments about careers in marine activities as you consider the many career options.

1. Are you interested in a career on the water? If so, you could be a commercial fisher. There is also the possibility of working in water transportation—from tugboats and ferries to ocean liners. Opportunities also exist in the Navy, Coast Guard, and Merchant Marine.

2. Does a career beneath the water appeal to you? A very small proportion of commercial fishing is conducted as diving operations. Divers can also enter commercial diving operations and do ship repair and pier and marina maintenance. Dive schools offer another career choice. And of course, there is also the possibility of service aboard a Navy submarine.

3. Do you want a career involving the study of oceans and other bodies of water? Aquatic biologists study plants and animals living in water. Marine biologists study saltwater organisms, while limnologists study freshwater organisms. Oceanographers study the physical characteristics of oceans and the ocean floor.

Find out more about a career in marine activities

The more contact you have with marine activities, the easier it will be for you to determine which one is most appealing to you. Also, you will want to contact these organizations for more career information.

For general information about fishing occupations:

National Oceanic and Atmospheric Administration, Office of Fisheries Conservation and Management
1335 East-West Highway
Silver Spring, MD 20910

For information about certified training programs for diving (umbilical) careers:

College of Oceaneering, International Dive School
272 South Fries Avenue
Wilmington, CA 90744

For information on merchant marine career, training, and licensing requirements:

Maritime Administration, U.S. Department of Transportation
400 7th Street, SW
Washington, DC 20590

For further information on oceanography:

American Society of Limnology and Oceanography
Virginia Institute of Marine Science
College of William and Mary
Glouster Point, VA 23062

CAREERS

IN

RECREATION

“T” he luckiest people in the world are those who get to do all year round what they most like to do during their summer vacation," according to Mark Twain. Some of these lucky people are nature lovers who have careers as recreation workers. The focus of their careers is to provide both adults and children with a memorable experience related to the outdoors. The experience could be as exotic as observing turtles in the Galapagos Islands or as ordinary as teaching archery in a summer

camp. Wherever they work, recreation workers plan, orga-
nize, and direct the offered activities.

What it's like to be a recreation worker

There is variety in being a recreation worker, enough variety to
match most nature lovers' specific
interests. You could be a camp
counselor; an ecotour guide; a
horseback-riding instructor; a
river rafter; a golf, tennis, or
swimming instructor; a ski pa-
troller; a sports team organizer;
a trek leader; a dude ranch manager; or a wilderness survival
instructor. Your workplace could
range from the wilderness to a
city park. You could work for the
government or for a private business or organization.

Let's find out what happens on the job

Whatever your job as a recreation worker is, you will probably
have the task of planning, orga-
nizing, and directing the activity.
A trek leader has to choose the
itinerary, arrange for the food
and lodging, and direct the day-
to-day operation of the trip. A ski
instructor has to plan his or her
lessons, schedule slopes, secure
the essential equipment, and
provide instruction. A camp
director has to plan and oversee
every aspect of a camp. Part
of your job always will be to
enhance people's appreciation of
nature and to foster their responsible use of the environment.

The pleasures and pressures of the job

As a recreation worker, you have the opportunity to share your appreciation of some aspect of nature with others. At a summer camp, you might be introducing a young child to canoeing or camp-outs. At a dude ranch, you could be sharing your interest in horses with both adults and children. At all times, you will have responsibility for the safety of the individuals with whom you are sharing the recreational activity. This can be a very weighty task if you are leading a tour or trek into a foreign country or the wilderness. You also have the pressure of directing the activity.

The rewards, the pay, and the perks

Your benefits go beyond your pay because you have the opportunity to work outdoors and enjoy nature. Unfortunately, the jobs of many recreational workers are seasonal. In 1993, the average salary for all full-time recreation professionals was $30,000 according to the National Recreation and Park Association. Your salary could be as low as $22,000 to as high as $95,000, depending on your level of responsibility and the size of the staff. Most full-time recreation workers receive vacation and other benefits, while part-time workers receive few, if any, benefits.

Getting started

It is possible to get a job as a recreation worker with a high school diploma, or sometimes less, for many summer jobs. But if you want a full-time professional position, you will usually need to have a college degree with a major in parks and recreation or leisure studies. For many jobs, a bachelor's degree in any liberal arts major may be all you need. In order to secure an administrative position, you will find a master's degree in parks and recreation or related fields helpful. To get any position as a recreation worker, it is a good idea to get certification from the National Recreation and Park Association showing your education and experience on the professional, provisional, or technical level.

Climbing the career ladder

Your education level will usually play a part in your advancement; however, you can advance with only a high school diploma. Also, the higher you climb, the less you will work directly with nature. Beginning as a recreation worker, you can climb the ladder to recreation leader in charge of programs, then to a recreation center director. You could then advance to recreation supervisor responsible for all recreation in an area and finally to director of parks and recreation in a city or county.

Now decide if being a recreational worker is right for you

You will have the opportunity to channel your love of nature into one of many career choices. Think now about the type of job that you would like to have as a recreation worker. "I would like to have a job that involves _____."

1. working with children
2. working with adults
3. working in the wilderness
4. working in an urban area
5. traveling to foreign countries
6. considerable adventure
7. teaching a skill
8. managing a recreational facility
9. sports or sports teams
10. vacation excursions

After you know your job preferences, you are ready to explore exactly which careers are the right fit for you.

Things you can do to get a head start

The demand for seasonal recreation workers is great. Because many of these jobs are filled by high school and college students, you can start building experience as a recreation worker while you are still in school. You can also make yourself a more attractive candidate for a job by getting certification of certain skills, especially swimming instructor, lifeguard, first aid, and CPR.

Let's Meet...

Peggy Day
Trek Leader

Peggy leads treks to exotic locales and has walked from one end of the Himalayas to the other.

Tell me how you got started in a career in tourism.

I was talking to an architect who was working on a tourism project in Nepal about being a housesitter. A bad storm came in and knocked out the power and water so I had to stay overnight. In the morning when he awoke, he found that I'd gotten a bucket of water from a stream and made breakfast over a campfire. He was so impressed with my initiative that he hired me as an assistant to work in Nepal studying the feasibility of hotels to which you could trek.

What special skills do you need to be a good trek leader?

Obviously, you need leadership skills—an understanding of how to handle people. You must also be able to think ahead and to stay in control of any situation. It's rather like being a parent who is looking out for the kids.

What do you like most about your job?

It gives me an opportunity to travel the world with people from all walks of life. Out on the trail, nothing matters except how you respond to the environment. Trekking has given me friends throughout the world because we have shared something so memorable together. The bond is incredible.

What special knowledge do you need to be a good trek leader?

It's important to know the customs and traditions of the country where you are trekking. For example, in Bhutan you always walk to the left of religious shrines. It's also helpful to know some of the native language.

Is there a lot of competition for jobs as a trek leader?

Initially, there is a tremendous amount of competition for a job as a trek leader. However, most people prefer more permanence in their lives, so an experienced leader finds it easier to get jobs.

Who employs trek leaders?

You may work for a travel company, or you may work independently leading tours for several companies. You can also create and sell your own tours.

An Expert Trekker in Bhutan

Peggy has a broad background of experience in trekking in the Himalayas; however, she decided to focus on Bhutan, a small independent country that lies between India and Tibet. The country is not as well-traveled, and so there is less competition for tours. She has led many treks to Bhutan and speaks some of the native language.

In putting together a trek in Bhutan, she has to devise the itinerary, arrange air travel and land accommodations, secure visas, and contact the Bhutanese who will help her with the trek. There is never any confusion when one person organizes the entire trip.

A typical trek lasts from 1 to 3 weeks. They walk and hike while looking for wildlife and admiring the magnificent scenery. Most of the trek is usually on trails from 7,000 to 13,000 feet in elevation. Pack animals carry their supplies for camping out. On the lower levels, horses are used, but higher up they use yaks. Native Bhutanese care for the animals. Also accompanying the trekkers is a cook and helpers as well as a representative of a Bhutan tour company. It is essential to have someone with the group who knows the land and the people in order not to make any awkward or embarrassing mistakes.

Let's Meet...

Joy Gallaway
Camp Director

Joy believes that she belongs out-of-doors in the mountains. During the school year, she is a classroom teacher, but every summer she directs a resident camp.

Tell me how you got started in resident camping.

At 17, I was looking for a job away from home for the summer. I applied to be a camp counselor at a local church camp in Salt Lake City. At that time, I had never been to camp and had no idea what to expect. The camp director who hired me had been involved in camping for 30 years. I really respected her and aspired to have her job one day. Four years later, I directed that camp and have been doing camp administration work ever since.

What special skills do you need to be a good camp director?

Enthusiasm and diplomacy are most important. Being a camp director is mainly being a good role model. My mood, energy level, confidence, and attitude tend to set the tone for the rest of the staff.

What do you like most about your job?

I like the last day of a camp session best when I see kids crying because they're "camp sick" and don't want to leave. This is the greatest affirmation that we have accomplished what we are here to do.

What do you like least about your job?

Being under a microscope. The staff tends to have midsummer burnout and question what the administrative staff members are doing. Every move is scrutinized.

Do you get to meet a lot of new people on the job?

Each year brings new staff members, and each session brings new campers. At the camp that I have been at for the past 4 years, we usually have seven international staff members each summer, and I have especially enjoyed meeting and learning from these people. The relationships formed at camp are stronger than even those formed in high school. You get to know people quickly because you are living in close quarters with them and are coming together on common ground.

What is your next career move likely to be?

I would really enjoy running an outdoor school during the times between camp. I love nature and belong outside all year.

What advice would you give young people starting out in resident camping?

Be enthusiastic. I can teach you how to build a fire or sing a camp song, but enthusiasm and energy have to come from within.

Camping and Personal Growth

If Joy were a tree and you were to study her growth rings, you would find the thickest rings—the times of most growth—have occurred during the summer when she was at camp. She has learned more about herself and the world around her at camp than at any other time in her life.

Joy's first camp director believed in giving people a chance. When Joy bounded into her office 10 years ago pleading for a job, she hired her even though she didn't think she'd last 2 weeks. After that first summer, she felt most at home at camp. She enrolled in first aid, CPR, and lifeguarding and completed a correspondence course in camp counseling so that she could return to camp the following summer with more skills. After several summers, Joy was old enough to run a camp. Her "rings" really grew that summer.

Today, Joy carries on her first camp director's tradition of "giving chances." Every summer she makes it a point to take a chance and hire three or four people in whom she sees a spark. She wants to give back what has been given to her. As long as Joy continues to learn and grow from the camping experience, she plans to return each summer because she feels that you can never have too many thick "growth rings" in your tree.

Success Stories

Frederick Gunn

Today, summer camp is an American tradition with more than 5 million children attending each summer. The "father" of the organized camp is Frederick Gunn, who is credited with establishing the first summer camp. In 1849 Gunn founded a boarding school for boys. During the Civil War, the students wanted to play soldier and sometimes slept outdoors on the ground, and at times would stay overnight at a nearby lake. In the summer of 1861, Gunn and his wife took the entire school for a 2-week stay on a beach. There the boys boated, sailed, fished, and hiked. The experience proved to be so enjoyable that it was repeated in 1863 and 1865. Then Gunn established a camp closer to the school on a lake. This camp remained in operation for 12 years until the school started having a summer break.

American Camping Association

Not long after the first summer camp was established, other organizations started camps. Then in 1910 the American Camping Association was founded. The organization's mission is to enhance the quality of the camp experience for youth and adults, to promote high professional practices in camp administration, and to interpret the values of camp to the public. Besides publishing a guide to accredited camps, it also accredits summer youth camps for health, safety, and program quality.

Find Out More

You and a career in recreation

An important part of succeeding in any career is having certain characteristics. They can be part of your personality or developed through experience. Here is a list of essential characteristics for recreation workers. How many of these characteristics do you have now? How many will you need to develop?

- Outgoing personality
- Good at motivating people
- Ability to get along well with people
- Sensitive to the needs of others
- Willingness to accept responsibility
- Ability to exercise good judgment
- Creativity and resourcefulness
- Ability to delegate tasks
- Attention to detail
- Patience
- Self-confidence
- Flexibility
- Leadership skills
- Solid communication skills
- A genuine liking of people

**Find out
more about
a career in
recreation**

Firsthand experience as a camp counselor, an intern, volunteer, or seasonal employee will give you a solid picture of what it's like to be a recreation worker. Certain organizations also have helpful career information. To find out about local government jobs in recreation, contact your nearest department of parks and recreation. Ordering information for materials describing careers and academic programs in recreation is available from:

National Recreation and Park
    Association
Division of Professional Services
2775 South Quincy Street
Suite 300
Arlington, VA 22206

American Association for Leisure
    and Recreation
1900 Association Drive
Reston, VA 22209

American Camping Association
5000 State Road 67 North
Martinsville, IN 46151-7902

You will also find it helpful to read *Opportunities in Recreation and Leisure Careers* written by Clayne R. Jensen and Jay H. Naylor and published by VGM Career Horizons.

CAREERS IN THE PARK SYSTEMS

W hile everyone is able to enjoy today's parks, the first parks were set aside as hunting areas for royalty and the nobility in ancient Egypt and Rome. Today, a park can be in a historical setting like Gettysburg or the Statue of Liberty, in majestic mountains like Yosemite and the Grand Tetons, in a seashore or on a lake in your state, or in your own community. Altogether there are more than 100,000 national, state,

71

and community parks. And within these parks are jobs for many people, including rangers.

What it's like to be a ranger

You will have two main responsibilities. The first is to ensure the safety of all visitors to the park, and the second is to protect the park and all its natural inhabitants from inappropriate use by the visitors. Rangers are also expected to introduce visitors to the natural and cultural history of a park. Another responsibility is to help maintain the park. Conservation of the natural resources in a park is yet another part of a ranger's job.

Let's find out what happens on the job

Your exact tasks as a ranger will depend on the type of job you hold and the park where you work. Many rangers work in **law enforcement,** seeing that all laws and regulations are being followed. Here, your duties might include patrolling the waters of a lake or a ski slope. Other rangers work as **naturalists** or intepreters, explaining the wonders of the park to visitors, answering their questions, and preparing programs. **Administrative** work is also necessary. Visitor permits have to be issued; records have to be kept; public relations have to be handled; and budgets have to be followed. In addition, park employees must be supervised.

Ranger duties may involve **maintenance,** such as maintaining and building roads, trails, and facilities. **Conservation** work includes studying and protecting the park's ecosystem. The work in some big parks like Yosemite and Yellowstone may offer many of the same jobs as running a city.

The work can be hazardous. Rangers must serve as firefighters and participate in search and rescue missions. Some rangers become specialists in one area such as mountain rescue, avalanche control, or park flora and fauna.

The pleasures and pressures of the job

Here is a job that seems to be ideal for the individual who wishes to be closely involved with nature and work outdoors. You are sharing the special natural features of a park with its visitors and conserving the park for future generations of visitors. And you are working in a unique setting that has been set aside because it contains great virgin forests, majestic mountains, active volcanoes, a desert, a historical landmark, or some other important feature.

If downsides exist in this job, there aren't many. During a park's busiest season, you may find yourself working longer than the typical 40-hour week. It is also possible that you will be exposed to dangerous work like firefighting and rescue missions. And some parks can be so crowded in season that their natural beauty is greatly diminished.

The rewards, the pay, and the perks

The special camaraderie rangers have adds to their overall job enjoyment. If you are a ranger working for the National Park Service, Bureau of Land Management, or U.S. Corps of Engineers, you will usually start at the GS-5 to GS-7 level depending on your education and experience. You will receive a generous benefits package including health and life insurance, paid vacations and holidays, sick leave, and pension plans. Your salary and benefits will be comparable if you are employed as a ranger in a state, county, or municipal park.

Getting started

To work as a ranger, whether it is for the federal, state, county, or municipal government, usually requires having a bachelor's degree in parks and recreation management. More than 300 colleges offer programs in this area, and more than 90 programs have been accredited by the National Recreation and Park Association. If you get your degree in another field, you must take at least 24 semester units of park recreation and management courses or related disciplines. Without a degree, you'll need 3 years of work experience in parks or conservation. Also, it is possible to get a job as a ranger with some combination of college education and experience. One way to document your education and experience qualifications is to become certified by the National Recreation and Park Association.

Climbing the career ladder

Most rangers start in entry-level positions and then begin their climb up the career ladder. Almost every position is filled through the promotion of current rangers. Your first move up the career ladder will be to head park ranger, park manager, or district supervisor; or you may decide to branch off into a specialization like park planning or resource management. From this point, you can move into district, regional, or headquarters administration positions.

Now decide if being a ranger is right for you

Are you ready to face the stiffest competition imaginable to become a ranger? For every applicant that succeeds in getting a job with the National Park Service, 100 qualified applicants fail to get a job. While the competition is slightly less intense on the state, county, and municipal levels, it is still quite impressive. Wherever you apply for a job, it is important to have acquired the widest possible skills, including a knowledge of first aid and CPR, law enforcement, forestry, and wildlife management, to make yourself a more attractive job candidate. Are you willing to acquire these skills?

Let's Meet...

Shelton Johnson
Ranger Naturalist

Shelton follows in the tradition of John Muir. His interests are nature, the arts, and creative writing.

Is a career as a ranger naturalist something you always dreamed about?

No. As an inner-city African-American child, I had never camped, hiked, or visited a national park. My upbringing was strictly urban, primarily in Detroit. My first wilderness experience was in the tropical rain forest in West Africa when I was in the Peace Corps, but I always had been fascinated by the natural world.

What first attracted you to a career as a ranger?

When I was in graduate school working on my master's in creative writing and poetry, I decided to spend the summer working in Yellowstone because I thought that I would have time for my writing. In my off-duty hours, I started to learn about the park through reading, hiking, and backpacking. The next summer, I worked in the park again for the concessionaire and began to understand some of

the day-to-day operations of the park. These experiences convinced me that I wanted a career involving wilderness, so I applied for a position as a seasonal ranger at Yellowstone National Park and was accepted.

What is involved in applying for a position as a national park ranger?

I first applied to be a seasonal ranger. To do this, you fill out an application form for two national parks. The West Entrance Supervisor was impressed with my work experience at Yellowstone and my educational background so I was accepted as a seasonal ranger. It can be difficult to get permanent, full-time status as a ranger. It has taken as long as 10 seasons for some employees to pass this hurdle! I did it in my fourth season.

Describe a typical day at work.

My day begins at 11:30 a.m. when I come to the Visitor Center at Yosemite National Park where I now work. At first, my time is spent doing program development work and handling mail and correspondence. Then I work in the Visitor Center for several hours answering questions ranging from the closest restroom to the name of the flower or bird a visitor saw on a walk. Plus, I may have to fix audio-visual equipment, help people find a place to stay, and in general orient people to their new surroundings. Next, I prepare for my nature walk and then lead a 90-minute walk. It's back for another session at the Visitor Center before I lead another 90-minute walk to end my workday.

Shelton's First Experiences as a Ranger

Shelton's career began as a seasonal park ranger at the busy West Entrance Ranger Station in Yellowstone National Park. Being a gate ranger involved taking money, selling passes, issuing permits, and answering all kinds of questions even though 70 cars were waiting behind the questioner to get in the park.

In his second year at the gate, he also worked as a firefighter on the North Fork and Fan Fires that burned thousands of acres in Yellowstone.

The next season he worked in the Superintendent's Office in public affairs, where one of his jobs was to take the media on naturalist tours as a follow-up on the fire.

When he obtained permanent status, his job shifted to the Chief Ranger's Office where his duties were primarily clerical. But in the winter, Shelton had the challenge and excitement of delivering the mail on a snowmobile on a 150-mile route on which he experienced nature at its best and worst. He encountered bison, coyotes, and other wildlife, and dealt with snowstorms. One winter's day, as he descended into Hayden Valley, it was more than 60° below zero.

His last position at Yellowstone was as park naturalist interpreting natural history for visitors.

Let's Meet...

Bob Kanagaki
Naturalist

Bob is a ranger naturalist at the Black Diamond Mines Regional Preserve, which features a coal mine.

Tell me how you got started.

I discovered Black Diamond while working in an archaeology field class as an undergraduate and began hiking at the park after I graduated. I worked in business for several years after college but grew weary of the routine and being confined indoors. I decided to return to school for an advanced degree and possibly a teaching credential. While in graduate school, I found a position as a student aide at Black Diamond. I knew nothing of interpreting natural history when I took the position but found that I enjoyed it because it allowed me to combine my interest in natural and cultural history with my liking for outdoor work.

Did you need any special schooling or training?

In this park district, interpreters (naturalists) must have a bachelor's degree in a related field, such as a natural science discipline or cultural history plus experience in the field. I received my training and

first experiences in interpretation when I
worked as a student aide and temporary
naturalist. Some of the information I present
in programs today comes from what I learned
in college. However, the more specialized
information, such as mining history and technology, came from coworkers.

What do you like most about your job?

I enjoy my job because it doesn't have a set
daily routine. No two days are ever the same
because we conduct such a wide variety of
programs (geology hikes, mining history talks,
wildflower walks, snake talks, bicycle or canoe
tours, and slide shows). Also, we have a wide
variety of other duties, including writing
articles for publications, planning and conducting special events such as concerts, monitoring
wildlife, and preparing artifact displays. This
job is especially satisfying when I can introduce people to the natural beauty of the park
or to new ideas or concepts. I enjoy hearing the
"Oooohs!" when I have shown people something that they've never seen before or when
they link something I have said about the park
to information they already have.

Do you get to meet a lot of new people on the job?

I meet an incredible variety of people, and they
provide much of my satisfaction in the job.
Many have never visited the park before and
want to find out more about it. I also like that
these visitors are at the park to enjoy them-
selves and get away from other concerns.

How Bob Got a Naturalist Job

In Bob's district, openings for naturalist positions are distributed to park offices, employment offices, and college placement centers by the Personnel Department. Applicants must submit a complete job application form and supplemental statements detailing their experience in various types of interpretation.

The applications are reviewed by a screening panel and qualified applicants are placed into two hiring pools with all applicants in the first pool getting interviews. The panel asks questions to clarify each applicant's knowledge and experience and to determine the applicant's suitability. To determine the quality of the applicant's work, each is asked to give a 5-minute interpretive presentation before the panel on a topic of his or her choice.

The top candidates then take a field test in the park for which they are applying; this test allows the supervising naturalists to check the depth and breadth of the candidate's knowledge and experience in an area where he or she is likely to work if hired. The final candidate is usually chosen after the field test.

The Personnel Department then conducts a background check before offering the position to this candidate.

Success Stories

Theodore Roosevelt

Theodore Roosevelt can be described as the first President of the United States to be truly interested in conservation. As a young boy he became fascinated by nature, and Roosevelt and his cousins formed the "Roosevelt Museum of Natural History" and kept their collection of bones, dead mice, stones, and other objects in a dresser drawer. When he became President in 1901, one of the major parts of his program was conservation of natural resources. Roosevelt loved the Far West and wanted to conserve its great forests and wildlife. He removed 150 million acres of timberland from sale and turned this land into national forests. Roosevelt also brought water to the dry Western lands through 25 irrigation projects. Then in 1908 he held a White House conference on the conservation of national resources. This led to the establishment of a National Conservation Commission and many state commissions.

Smoke Jumpers

After World War I, the forest service became interested in the use of airplanes in its fire control activities. At first, airplanes were used for fire detection. Then they began to be used to supply firefighters and to drop water and chemical bombs on fires. In 1939 parachutists called "smoke jumpers" began to leap into remote areas to fight fires. Today, these highly trained jumpers play a vital role in controlling forest fires.

Find Out More

You and a career as a ranger

Many people have glamorous visions of what the job of ranger entails. They only see the job as a wonderful opportunity to work in a fabulous natural setting. The next time you go to a park, carefully observe the activities of the rangers. Also, if the opportunity arises, try to talk to the rangers about their duties. After you have talked to several rangers, you'll have a more realistic view of the job and its duties. If the job of ranger still appeals to you after learning more about it, answer the following questions to determine if you have the right kind of personality to handle this job.

1. Rangers may work with park visitors.
   - Are you tactful and courteous?
   - Are you patient with people?
   - Could you politely answer the same questions you have heard hundreds of times before?
   - Do you genuinely enjoy talking to people?
   - Do you like meeting new people?
   - Do you have a sense of humor?

2. Rangers may face dangerous situations.

- Do you have a cool head in emergencies?
- Are you courageous?
- Are you confident in your ability to handle emergencies?

3. Rangers may be involved in conservation efforts.

- Do you believe in the importance of conserving and protecting the natural resources in parks?

4. Rangers may be involved in supervising park workers.

- Are you an organized person?
- Are you a good persuader?

5. Rangers may do routine administrative tasks.

- Are you self-motivated?
- Can you handle details well?

Find out more about being a ranger

To find out more about being a ranger, you may want to contact these organizations:

National Recreation and Park
    Association
2775 South Quincy Street
Suite 300
Arlington, VA 22206

U.S. Department of the Interior
National Park Service
1849 C Street, NW
Washington, DC 20240

INDEX